An Applied Alternatives, LLC Project
www.appliedalternatives.com

LIMITLESS

First Edition: August 2011.
Printed in the United States of America
ISBN: 978-0-615-52727-7

LIMITLESS

To My Wife and Children,

Forever bound by a sutra of love.

Limitlessly devoted to you,

Dad

Limitless
by
Glenn Short

Once upon a time there
was an idea and the idea
was said to be a circle.

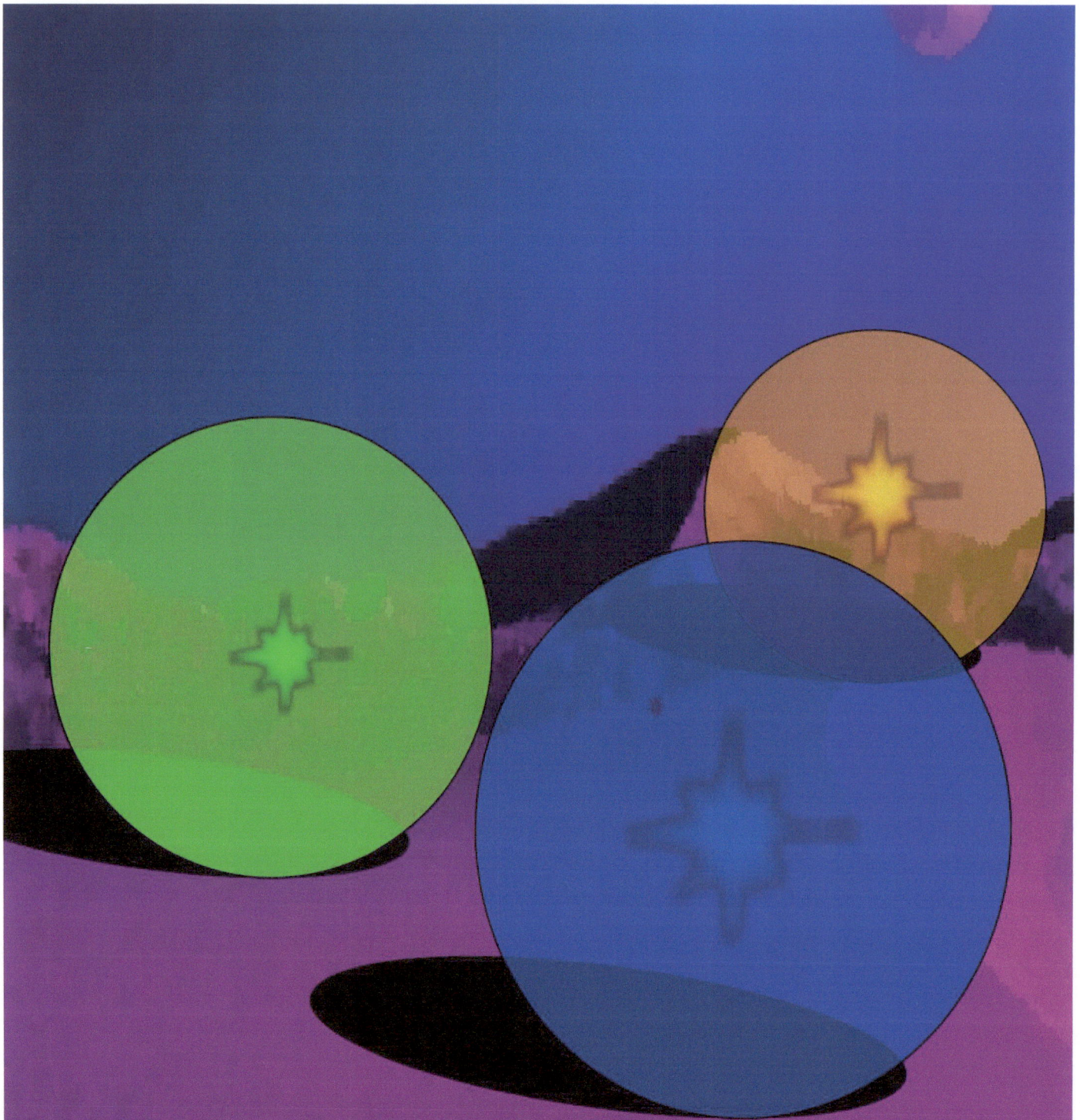

And there were several
different colors and sizes of
the same idea.

And on the other side of the
world, the same idea existed and
the idea was said to be a square.

Many different sizes and colors
shared the idea of the square.

The same idea existed on another side of the world and they called it a triangle.

There were many sizes and shades of color that followed the idea of the triangle.

Likewise, where the circle lived, there also existed an idea that was called a rectangle.

The idea of the
rectangle was also
shared by different
colors and sizes.

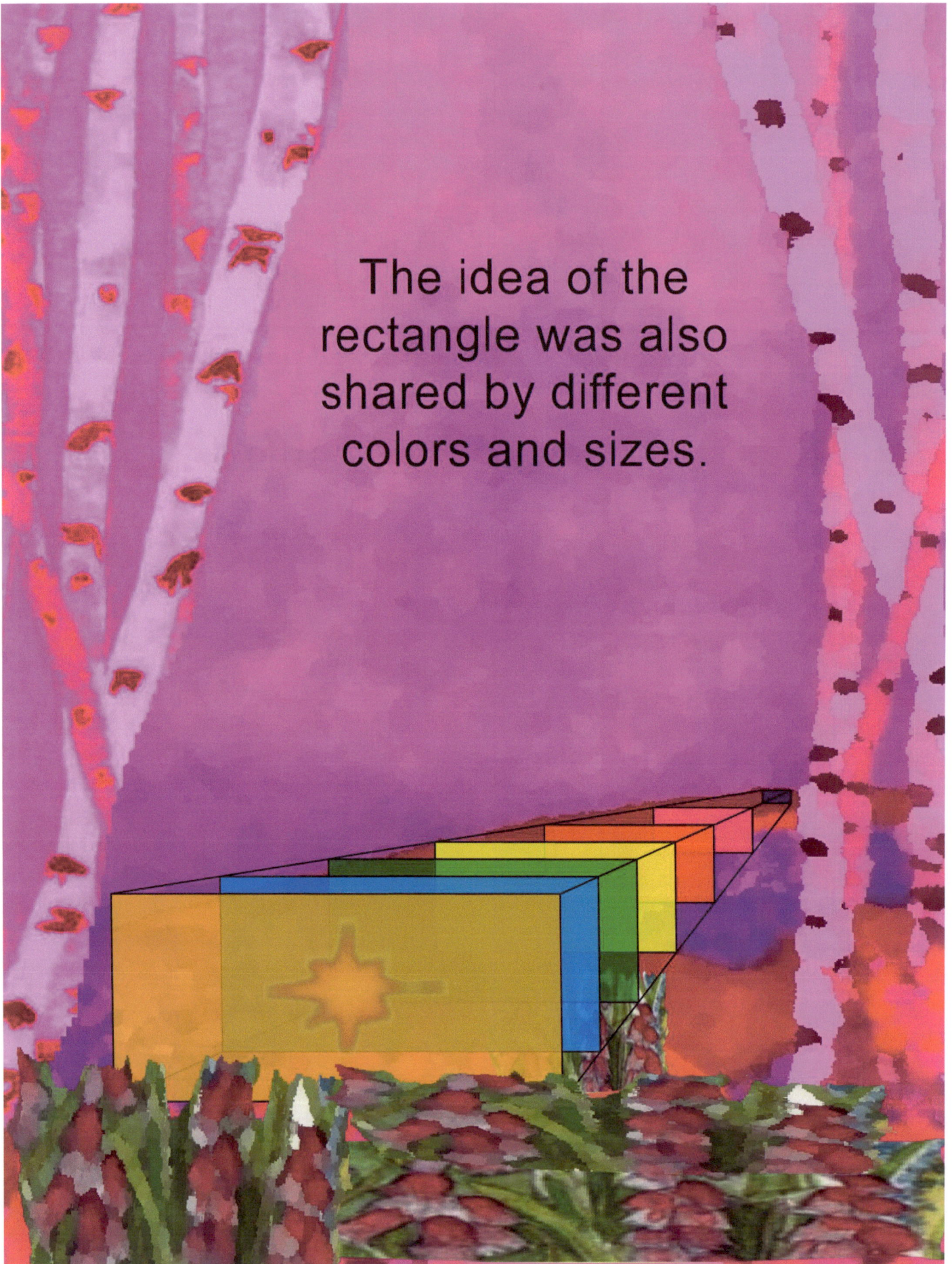

On the opposite side of the earth
that lived the square, a different
and older idea lived and they
called it an Octagon.

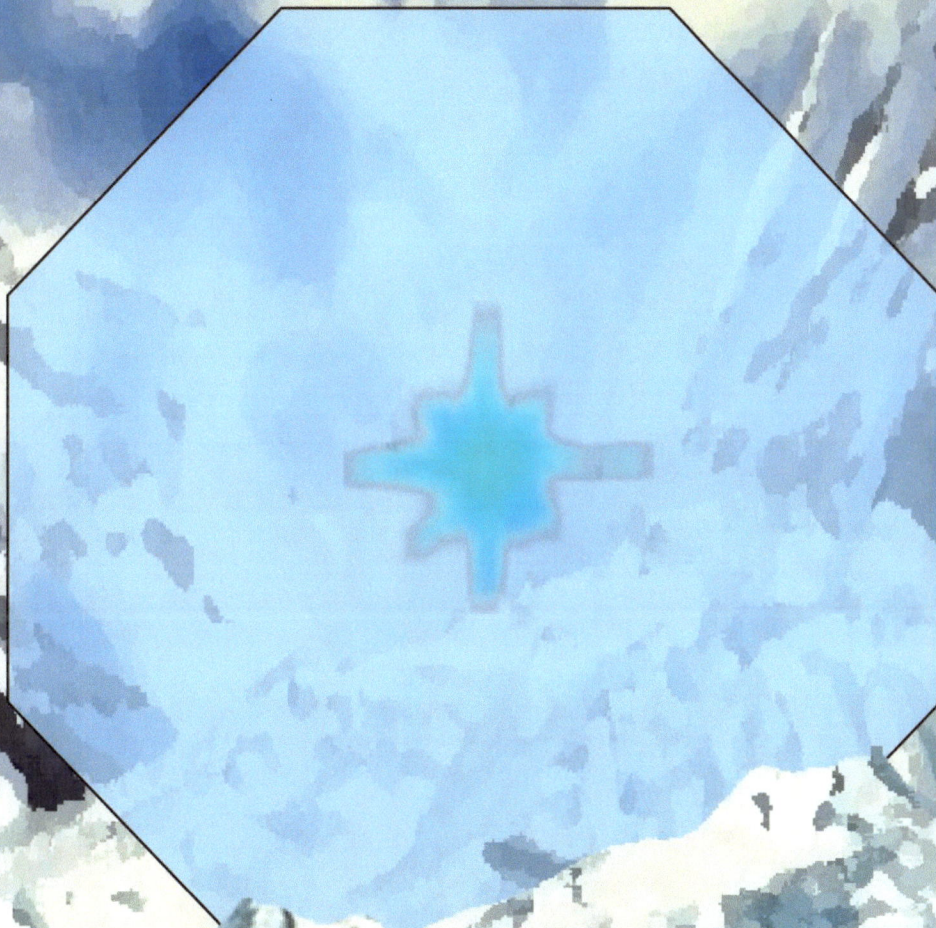

The Octagon also had
followers of different sizes
and colors.

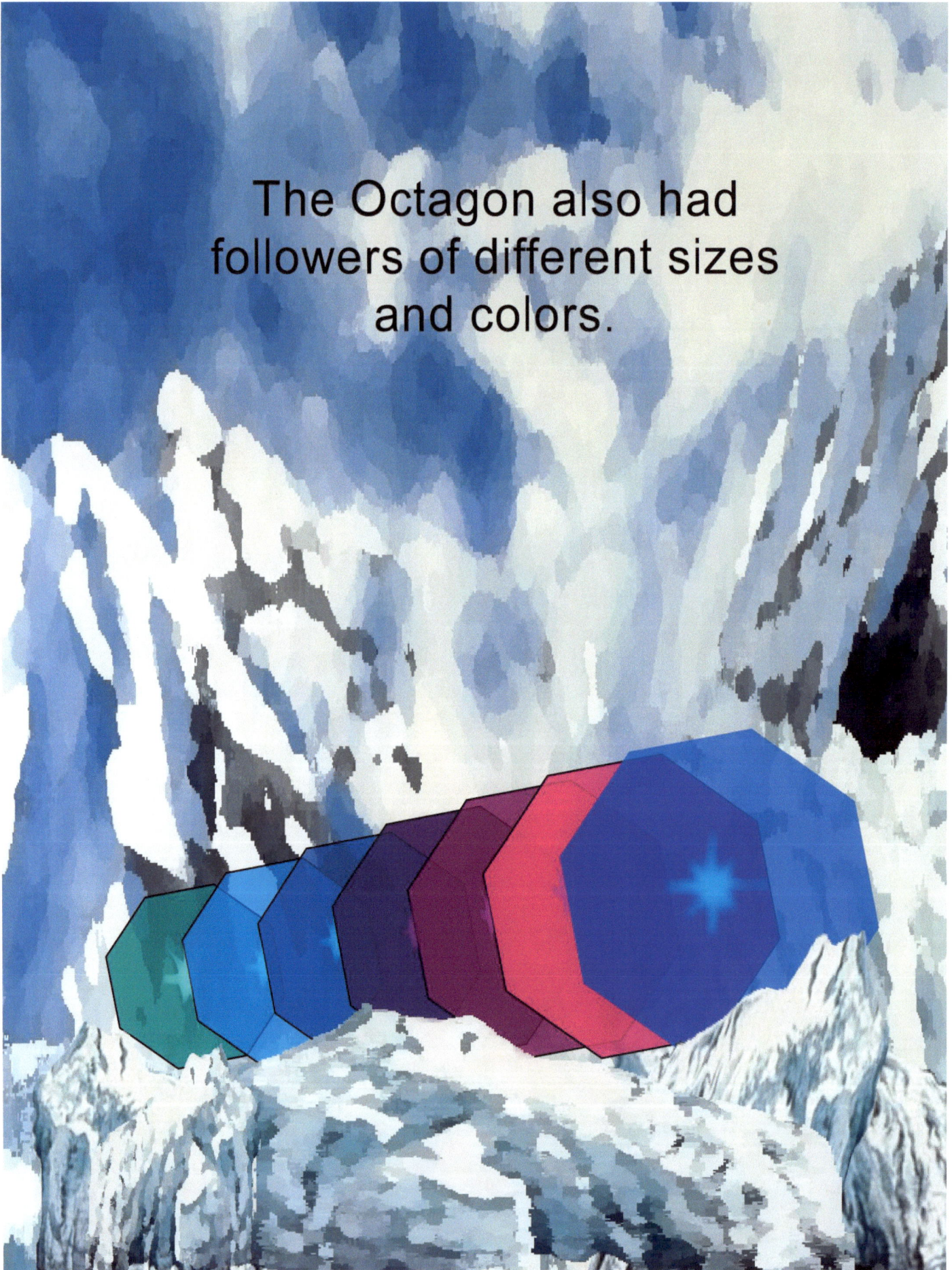

Where the triangle lived there also existed the idea of the pentagon.

And as you would know it,
pentagons of all sizes and colors
lined up to follow that idea.

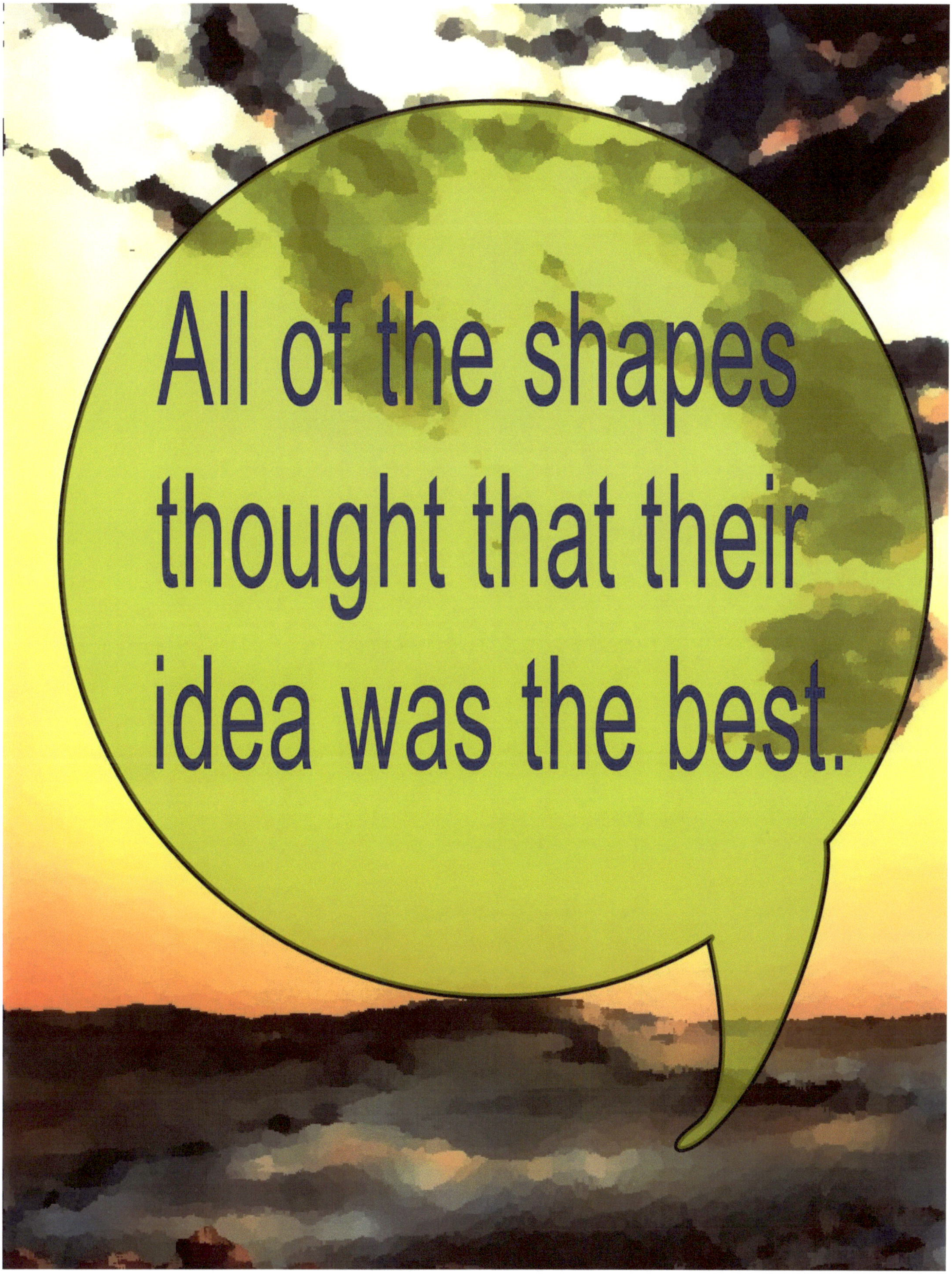
All of the shapes thought that their idea was the best.

The circle said that everyone needed to live the way of the circle because it was the best idea.

While the square showed off it's edges and bragged that it was the best shape and idea.

The rectangle said, "I am kind of like the square, but have longer sides to the idea, so I am better."

The pentagon said, "my angles are similar to the triangle, rectangle and square, but, I have a more unique Idea, shape, and name."

The octagon said
from the mountain
tops, "my shape is
like all of the others,
but, I have more
sides to my shape
and my name
sounds the best!"

All of the ideas called for a meeting
to decide which idea should be
called the best. From all over the
world, ideas of all colors, shapes
and sizes came together to decide...

When the ideas came together something very sad happened. Not only did they begin comparing their idea to others, but they began comparing their size and color with all the other shapes, including their own. Their world went dark and the colors lost their inner glow.

The ideas fought for hours and they even began to lose their shape. The ideas couldn't even recognize themselves because their very idea took on a much different meaning. It was very sad and very dark.

Still in darkness...

They all agree that they needed a judge to decide which one was the best color, idea and shape of them all.

Then appeared an idea that was without shape. The shapeless shape was called by the other shapes to settle their differences. And there was darkness no more...

It was a shape without shape and a form without form. It was both large and small and it had shades of different colors about it.

With a great warmth the shapeless shape said, "Each and every one of you is focusing on the outer edges of your existence." Instead...

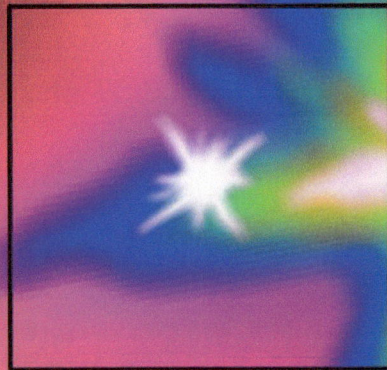

"...you should be focusing on the space in between the edges of your shape. The center of your idea is what matters, no matter what color, size or shape."

"The space in between is without shape which is the same as my shape and I am the Judge that you called upon to help", said the shapeless shape.

The edges were then dissolved and the once different shapes were able to talk to one another without judgment. There was now a Central Focus. And that Central Focus felt great. It was the warmth of love.

The Judge said, "that which has form is limited, it is limited to it's form. That which has no form is LIMITLESS. Love is at the center of all our shapes and ideas and once you remove the form, and focus on love, then there are no boundaries and love can only continue to grow."

All of the ideas were now happy and believed that love was at the center of their lives. There was a new found closeness to one another and a special closeness to the Judge.

As they all went their separate ways, the now formless shapes asked the Judge, "Who are you?"

The Judge responded with great devotion, "I am that I am, I am

LIMITLESS LOVE...

I am in all of you, no matter what color, size, or shape. Many that have lived call me God."

THE END